Readings in Sociology

Sources and Comment

SOCIOLOGY SERIES
Edited by John F. Cuber

John F. Cuber   *Peggy B. Harroff*

THE OHIO STATE UNIVERSITY

Readings in Sociology

Sources and Comment

NEW YORK

APPLETON-CENTURY-CROFTS, INC.

PRINTED IN THE UNITED STATES OF AMERICA
E - 24524

Preface

The "source book," or "readings book," as it is currently called, has become an established part of the paraphernalia of collegiate education. The study of original source materials is, of course, as old as education itself. But somewhere along the democratization route emphasis moved away from extensive reliance upon source materials in favor of the much-maligned, and sometimes deservedly so, "textbook." The textbook's obvious advantage of "balance," consistency in point of view and level of difficulty, and ready orientation to the real or assumed special needs of special categories of students, has not been without its consequent deficiencies. Textbook writing is notoriously unimaginative, pedestrian, and sometimes simply "bad." Profound and comprehensive ideas, it is often said, are sometimes oversimplified and, what is even worse, ideas unpalatable to the textbook writer have not infrequently been presented as straw men, readily demolished by the "huff and puff" of the most mediocre sort. Textbooks are sometimes written in such an unchallenging manner that, for the more advanced students at least, they constitute little intellectual adventure. Many teachers have resolved the textbook vs. source materials dilemma by trying both —the textbook for ease of comprehension, organization of the materials, and the presentation of a sustained point of view, and assigned library readings to acquaint the student with original contributions of noteworthy people, for amplification of certain materials, concreteness, sharpening of controversial issues, and sometimes as interest stimulators.

But the mechanics have not always worked out so well. The most serious current difficulty centers around the abysmal inadequacy of library facilities. Elementary courses in sociology, even in the smaller schools, tend to run in the hundreds, and in the larger institutions in the thousands. Libraries possess neither the necessary duplicate copies nor the reading room space to accommodate these large numbers, all seeking the same fifteen pages on the same day! A number of readings books are on the market, but the cost of the conventional text plus one of these readings books constitutes a book expenditure for a single course which often exceeds the cost conventions to which teachers and students have been accustomed.

It has occurred to us, then, that there is a place for a modestly priced book of readings which would supplement any of the currently used textbooks and still hold total course cost to a reasonable level. We doubt that many students would seriously object to a small expenditure for over 300 pages of "outside reading" which will save them countless hours of waiting in line and "fighting the library bureaucracy" for materials on "closed reserve."

In the selection of the readings to be included in this book we have utilized certain criteria. Obviously every reading does not meet every criterion, but in order to be included each had to meet a number of them and violate few.

(1) *Classics.* We sought a fair representation of classics— excerpts from a number of the books which are generally acknowledged to constitute the historical foundations of the discipline, such as *The Grammar of Science* or *Folkways.* The intention here is *not to exhaust but rather to illustrate* the category.

(2) *Readability.* However important the work or profound the idea or influential the man, there seems little merit in assigning readings which experience has demonstrated can be comprehended only by the occasional exceptional student. While we do not wish to appear to underestimate the capacities of today's collegians, there seems little point to being unrealistic about the competency level of the majority. We have included, however, readings which are difficult—in a few cases possibly "beyond" the comprehension of the larger bulk of the freshman population. But "a man's reach should exceed his grasp" and the effort of the successful will, we hope, be rewarded.

(3) *Interest.* Other things being anywhere near equal, we have chosen readings which experience has indicated are

interesting to students. If students are to continue beyond the elementary course, or possibly to become professional sociologists, their interest needs to be quickened by first hand knowledge of at least some of the more exciting things which professionals in the field have brought forth—either via empirical research or via imaginative construction.

(4) *Variety.* We have tried to present not only a variety of topics but also a variety of forms of sociological thought and even a variety of sources from which the readings have been selected. Thus, we have sampled a doctoral dissertation and unpublished manuscripts as well as the traditional articles and books.

(5) *Balance.* Although the more doctrinaire would sometimes prefer it otherwise, simple honesty requires that the student be acquainted with the fact that there are rather marked *differences* in the points of view and professional efforts of comparably ranking sociologists. We have tried to concretize this in the selections presented.

(6) *Empirical Research.* At least five selections are formally designed research studies presented in the familiar terms of "hypothesis, design, findings," and so on. Tabular data are reproduced *in toto* in three cases. This should enable more careful, critical presentation of actual studies and of our current procedures.

In assessing the merits of the individual selections, it is obvious that an element of arbitrariness was used. Suppose, for example, that we find a contemporary statement of the concept *mores* more readable than Sumner's. Shall we use the classic or the more efficient statement? Either could be justified. In some instances we chose the classic, even if a more readable paraphrasing were available. But by no means always.

The organization of a book of readings presents problems even more knotty than does the conventional textbook. Our final decision was to present a minimum of organization, presenting the sources in the three conventional categories of "culture," "personality," and "society" with an added orientation section. This should make the readings book about equally adaptable to any existing textbook and allow the teacher maximum choice in collating readings and textbook. The book has been deliberately planned so that the teacher may use his individuality and his own thinking in presenting the material to best advantage. A given reading—something on "national character" for instance—may with almost equal logic be integrated into a unit on culture or personality or society. It is doubtful whether teachers would use all of the readings and even more doubtful that any one would use them in the order in which someone else may have assembled them.

There has been a certain logic in our process of excerpting. Some readings are shorter than has been conventional in the larger books of readings. In the interest of presenting more readings and introducing more authors and works, many of the readings have been considerably shortened, with apparently little or no loss in their functionality to the beginning student. Moreover, interest for this level, we have found, can be kept somewhat higher by eliminating some of the abstract, professional level *obiter dicta* which frequently are included in source materials.

Finally, we have written introductions to each section and also to each reading, which are designed to accomplish various purposes—to orient the student to the purpose of the reading or to the historical period from which it came or to some special aspect of the author's point of view, accomplishments, or place in the emergence of the profession. Sometimes questions are asked which are intended to focus the student's attention.

No attempt has been made to present a "Who's Who" of sociological worthies. It will be noted, for example, that some preeminent sociologists are not represented at all. Other relatively obscure ones are included. Since this is not a history of sociological thinking nor oriented to a course designed to train professionals, no such obligation would appear necessary. There is, nonetheless, a wide variety of contributors, sources, and selections, which we hope will prove useful and efficient as an aid to the classroom teaching of elementary sociology.

JFC
PBH

Columbus, Ohio

Contents

ix

PART II

PART III

PART IV

Part One

TRADITIONS AND ISSUES

Sociology, like all fields of knowledge, has a history as well as a present status among the family of disciplines. Sociology emerged out of philosophy in its theoretical aspects and out of humanitarianism in its practical accent. Its philosophical origins were marked by two notable "breakthroughs," both well over a half-century ago. There were, of course, many other pioneers but only these two will be introduced here—Herbert Spencer (1820-1903) and Karl Pearson (1857-1936).

While Spencer's contributions were several, one for which we are certainly indebted is his delineation of a domain for social science.[1] He separated the universe into three categories, each of which constituted "a place in the sun" for various scientific fields and, theoretically at least, marked off some defensible limits among them. The "inorganic" refers, as the term implies, to the world of non-living things such as the planetary system, the structure of the earth, and the processes through which these are ever becoming. The "organic" refers, of course, to so-called living things—the flora and fauna which comprise the domain of the biological sciences. Then, said Spencer, there is over and beyond these a "super-organic" domain (distinctly not super*natural*) consisting for the most part of the products of man's existence —of his language systems, his art, his institutions, in short, what we now customarily call "culture." It may be that the choice of the term *super*-organic was an unfortunate one, because of its easy confusion with super*natural* and the possibility of its being understood

[1] It should be noted that he was anticipated by August Comte somewhat earlier.

as something mystical or ultimate in the scheme of things.

People sophisticated in the sciences in our time would be quick to question the divisibility of the universe into the three neat categories of the Spencerian system. Let us take, for example, the current concern with the effect of atomic radiation upon the germ plasm. This involves all three universes—the inorganic, organic, and super-organic. The use of atomic *fission* is super-organic, a human invention which utilizes inorganic matter, and has certain known and probably numerous unknown implications for the organic universe. Likewise, modern scientists are much less sure than Spencer that any line can be drawn between living and non-living matter. But these modern sophistications aside, a very real breakthrough must be credited to Spencer for having established a domain of academic inquiry, called the super-organic, and for having placed it in an essentially scientific framework along with the more traditional scientific disciplines.

Spencer was much less naive than some of our contemporaries about the difficulties involved in objectifying culture and human behavior so that we might truly achieve the intentions implied in the term social *science*. The selection on page 8, written in 1873, has a modern as well as an archaic ring. Every text dealing with the methodology and research techniques of the social sciences cautions the student about the hazards impeding the achievement of objectivity. To be sure, we have a number of inventions to reduce the grossness of some of the hazards, but they have by no means been eliminated, and the more truly sophisticated sociologists know this full well.

One of the specialties in the field of philosophy has come to be called the "philosophy of science." It is perhaps not so much a branch of philosophy as it is an application of philosophical concepts. It raises such questions as: What *is* science? How is scientific truth arrived at? And what are the limits within which it may be regarded as truth? Spencer, as well as many other early thinkers, touched upon problems of this sort, but one of the most articulate, clear and influential men was Karl Pearson, whose *Grammar of Science* has become almost a catechism of scientific sociology. The readings on pages 15 and 18, taken from the *Grammar of Science* (First Edition, 1892), are illustrative not only of modern dependence upon Pearsonian thinking but also of the unusual clarity of expression of a man who did not substitute obfuscation for profundity.

But there is much more to the sociological tradition than its scientific pretensions and achievements. From the beginning there have been at least three discernible groups of sceptics and critics. One group have denied, and still deny, that there can really be a science of the super-organic in any significant way resembling sciences in the older and stricter sense. A second group do not deny that there can *at some remote time* be such an achievement, but they feel that the problems of implementing scientific ambitions effectively are so great, the obstacles so vast, that to speak of social *science* glibly and optimistically for our time borders on pretension. Our naivete tends to make us too content, they say, with little important achievement and at the same time too complacent about the vast distance we have to go before there can be any important science of human behavior. Further, there is a third group who feel that a science of human and social behavior is possible and in considerable measure already achieved, but they are reluctant to limit sociological research and thinking to this kind of effort. They are mindful of the long and profound dependence of sociologists upon the humanities tradition: history, philosophy, linguistics. While acknowledging that sociology *can* be a science and *should* aspire to being better science, they lament the tendency to slough off the works of many men, both past and present, who do not choose to operate within a strict scientific set of criteria for their own research efforts. Robert Bierstedt (page 32) is one of these. His

almost poignant plea for preserving and using the tradition of humane letters is included here as a particularly
literate and responsible statement of the case. Throughout this book efforts to secure what are called "insights"
into some aspect of human nature or society will introduce the student to a considerable sample of this kind
of sociological endeavor.

The more recent history and condition of sociology
is discussed (page 43) in the excerpt from Roscoe and
Gisela Hinkle's *The Development of Modern Sociology,*
written in 1954. This reading is the concluding section
of their little book, in which they have with remarkable
clarity condensed and interpreted a vast amount of
historical research and writing.

Naive readers have sometimes concluded that the
inability of sociologists completely to agree among themselves concerning many questions of theory and research
is a reflection upon the authenticity of the content of
the discipline. Actually, no discipline is without disagreements among its professional practitioners. Nor should
it be. Progress can evolve only from innovation, and
innovation can be generated only out of doubt, disagree-
ment, or some other indication that someone sees something differently from the way in which someone else
does. Thus, the view is respectfully offered that the
sophisticated student of sociology should have a healthy
respect for the professional *disagreements* among the
practitioners of the art and science which goes by that
name. Moreover, it is also urged that competency, even
for the comparative beginner, should emerge out of an
appreciation and as thorough knowledge as possible of
different ways of seeing the sociological universe. A too
rigid, premature, and too glib consistency is, indeed,
"the hobgoblin of little minds."

Herbert Spencer

THE STUDY OF SOCIOLOGY *

Some of the more enthusiastic propagandists of social science in general, as well as sociologists in particular, have tended, in our opinion, to minimize the seriousness and pervasiveness of the difficulties which stand in the way of a true science of human behavior. While we would surely not contend that the difficulties are insurmountable, we do insist that they should be taken very seriously. It is interesting that Herbert Spencer, not far from a century ago, addressed himself to the same question to which careful philosophers of social science still find it necessary to direct themselves. Spencer's The Study of Sociology, from which this reading was taken, is much less widely quoted and discussed than some of his other works, but it does contain some challenging ideas, presented with clarity. Perhaps it is important, too, that these passages serve as an unpleasant reminder of both the ubiquity and the stubbornness of the obstacles to scientific achievement in sociology. The first part discusses the subject in more general terms, the other two single out for treatment two special categories of bias—those stemming from the student's class position and those, oddly enough, stemming from education itself. Those people who rely simply upon "education" as an antidote to prejudice may be a little startled to discover that almost 100 years ago, and no less so today, education itself can constitute a type of bias. Spencer is, of course, using education here in an inclusive sense. His treatment of the "two religions" is probably as accurate for the present as it was for his time, and certainly it is a provocative as well as original discussion.

* From Herbert Spencer, *The Study of Sociology* (New York, D. Appleton and Company, 1873), pp. 65-67, 219-220, 161-164.

7

DIFFICULTIES OF THE SOCIAL SCIENCE

From the intrinsic natures of its facts, from our own natures as observers of its facts, and from the peculiar relation in which we stand towards the facts to be observed, there arise impediments in the way of Sociology greater than those in the way of any other science.

The phenomena to be generalized are not of a directly-perceptible kind—cannot be noted by telescope and clock, like those of Astronomy; cannot be measured by dynamometer and thermometer, like those of Physics; cannot be elucidated by scales and test-papers, like those of Chemistry; are not to be got at by scalpel and microscope, like the less obvious biological phenomena; nor are to be recognized by introspection, like the phenomena Psychology deals with. They have severally to be established by putting together many details, no one of which is simple, and which are dispersed, both in Space and Time, in ways that make them difficult of access. Hence the reason why even cardinal truths in Sociology, such as the division of labour, remain long unrecognized. That in advanced societies men follow different occupations, was indeed a generalization easy to make; but that this form of social arrangement had neither been specially created, nor enacted by a king, but had grown up without forethought of any one, was a conclusion which could be reached only after many transactions of many kinds between men had been noted, remembered, and accounted for, and only after comparisons had been made between these transactions and those taking place between men in simpler societies and in earlier times. And when it is remembered that the data for the inference that labour becomes specialized, are far more accessible than the data for most other sociological inferences, it will be seen how greatly the advance of Sociology is hindered by the nature of its subject-matter.

The characters of men as observers, add to this first difficulty a second that is perhaps equally great. Necessarily men take with them into sociological inquiries, the modes of observation and reasoning which they have been accustomed to in other inquiries—those of them, at least, who make any inquiries worthy to be so called. Passing over the great majority

of the educated, and limiting ourselves to the very few who
consciously collect data, compare them, and deliberately draw
conclusions; we may see that even these have to struggle with
the difficulty that the habits of thought generated by converse
with relatively-simple phenomena, partially unfit them for converse with these highly-complex phenomena. Faculty of every
kind tends always to adjust itself to its work. Special adjustment
to one kind of work involves more or less non-adjustment to
other kinds. And hence, intellects disciplined in dealing with
less-involved classes of facts, cannot successfully deal with this
most-involved class of facts without partially unlearning the
methods they have learnt. From the emotional nature, too, there
arise great obstacles. Scarcely any one can contemplate social
arrangements and actions with the unconcern felt when con-
templating arrangements and actions of other kinds. For correct
observation and correct drawing of inferences, there needs the
calmness that is ready to recognize or to infer one truth as readily
as another. But it is next to impossible thus to deal with the
truths of Sociology. In the search for them, each is moved by
feelings, more or less strong, which make him eager to find this
evidence, oblivious of that which is at variance with it, reluctant
to draw any conclusion but that already drawn. And though
perhaps one in ten among those who think, is conscious that
his judgment is being warped by prejudice, yet even in him
the warp is not adequately allowed for. Doubtless in nearly
every field of inquiry emotion is a perturbing intruder: mostly
there is some preconception, and some *amour propre* that resists
disproof of it. But a peculiarity of Sociology is, that the emotions
with which its facts and conclusions are regarded, have unusual
strength. The personal interests are directly affected; or there is
gratification or offence to sentiments that have grown out of
them; or else other sentiments which have relation to the existing
form of society, are excited, agreeably or disagreeably.

And here we are introduced to the third kind of difficulty
—that caused by the position occupied, in respect to the phenomena to be generalized. In no other case has the inquirer to
investigate the properties of an aggregate in which he is himself
included. His relation towards the facts he here studies, we may
figure to ourselves by comparing it to the relation between a

single cell forming part of a living body, and the facts which
that living body presents as a whole. Speaking generally, the
citizen's life is made possible only by due performance of his
function in the place he fills; and he cannot wholly free himself
from the beliefs and sentiments generated by the vital con-
nexions hence arising between himself and his society. Here,
then, is a difficulty to which no other science presents anything
analogous. To cut himself off in thought from all his relationships
of race, and country, and citizenship—to get rid of all those
interests, prejudices, likings, superstitions, generated in him by
the life of his own society and his own time—to look on all the
changes societies have undergone and are undergoing, without
reference to nationality, or creed, or personal welfare; is what
the average man cannot do at all, and what the exceptional
man can do very imperfectly.

THE CLASS BIAS

Many years ago a solicitor sitting by me at dinner, complained
bitterly of the injury which the then lately-established County
Courts, were doing his profession. He enlarged on the topic in
a way implying that he expected me to agree with him in therefore condemning them. So incapable was he of going beyond
the professional point of view, that what he regarded as a
grievance he thought I also ought to regard as a grievance:
oblivious of the fact that the more economical administration of
justice of which his lamentation gave me proof, was to me, not
being a lawyer, matter for rejoicing.

The bias thus exemplified is a bias by which nearly all have
their opinions warped. Naval officers disclose their unhesitating
belief that we are in imminent danger because the cry for more
fighting ships and more sailors has not been met to their satisfac-
tion. The debates on the purchase-system proved how strong
was the conviction of military men that our national safety
depended on the maintenance of an army-organization like that
in which they were brought up, and had attained their respective

ranks. Clerical opposition to the Corn-Laws showed how completely that view which Christian ministers might have been
expected to take, was shut out by a view more congruous with
their interests and alliances. In all classes and sub-classes it is
the same. Hear the murmurs uttered when, because of the
Queen's absence, there is less expenditure in entertainments and
the so-called gaieties of the season, and you perceive that London
traders think the nation suffers if the consumption of super-
fluities is checked. Study the pending controversy about co-
operative stores *versus* retail shops, and you find the shop-
keeping mind possessed by the idea that Society commits a wrong
if it deserts shops and goes to stores—is quite unconscious that
the present distributing system rightly exists only as a means
of economically and conveniently supplying consumers, and
must yield to another system if that should prove more economical and convenient. Similarly with other trading bodies,
general and special—similarly with the merchants who opposed
the repeal of the Navigation Laws; similarly with the Coventry
weavers, who like free-trade in all things save ribbons.

The class-bias, like the bias of patriotism, is a reflex egoism;
and like it has its uses and abuses. As the strong attachments
citizens feel for their nation cause that enthusiastic cooperation
by which its integrity is maintained in presence of other nations,
severally tending to spread and subjugate their neighbours; so
the *esprit de corps* more or less manifest in each specialized
part of the body politic, prompts measures to preserve the integrity of that part in opposition to other parts, all somewhat
antagonistic.

THE EDUCATIONAL BIAS

It would clear up our ideas about many things, if we distinctly
recognized the truth that we have two religions. Primitive humanity has but one. The humanity of the remote future will
have but one. The two are opposed; and we who live midway
in the course of civilization have to believe in both.

These two religions are adapted to two conflicting sets of social requirements. The one set is supreme at the beginning; the other set will be supreme at the end; and a compromise has to be maintained between them during the progress from beginning to end. On the one hand, there must be social self-preservation in face of external enemies. On the other hand, there must be co-operation among fellow-citizens, which can exist only in proportion as fair dealing of man with man creates mutual trust. Unless the one necessity is met, the society disappears by extinction, or by absorption into some conquering society. Unless the other necessity is met, there cannot be that division of labour, exchange of services, consequent industrial progress and increase of numbers, by which a society is made strong enough to survive. In adjustment to these two conflicting requirements, there grow up two conflicting codes of duty; which severally acquire supernatural sanctions. And thus we get the two coexisting religions—the religion of enmity and the religion of amity.

Of course, I do not mean that these are both called religions. Here I am not speaking of names; I am speaking simply of things. Nowadays, men do not pay the same verbal homage to the code which enmity dictates that they do to the code which amity dictates—the last occupies the place of honour. But the real homage is paid in large measure, if not in the larger measure, to the code dictated by enmity. The religion of enmity nearly all men actually believe. The religion of amity most of them merely believe they believe. In some discussion, say, about international affairs, remind them of certain precepts contained in the creed they profess, and the most you get is a tepid assent. Now let the conversation turn on the "tunding" at Winchester, or on the treatment of Indian mutineers, or on the Jamaica business; and you find that while the precepts tepidly assented to were but nominally believed, quite opposite precepts are believed undoubtingly and defended with fervour.

Curiously enough, to maintain these antagonist religions, which in our transitional state are both requisite, we have adopted from two different races two different cults. From the books of the Jewish New Testament we take our religion of amity. Greek and Latin epics and histories serve as gospels for

our religion of enmity. In the education of our youth we devote
a small portion of time to the one, and a large portion of time
to the other. And, as though to make the compromise effectual,
these two cults are carried on in the same places by the same
teacher. At our Public Schools, as also at many other schools,
the same men are priests of both religions. The nobility of self-
sacrifice, set forth in Scripture-lessons and dwelt on in sermons,
is made conspicuous every seventh day; while during the other
six days, the nobility of sacrificing others is exhibited in glowing
words. The sacred duty of blood-revenge, which, as existing
savages show us, constitutes the religion of enmity in its primitive
form—which, as shown us in ancient literature, is enforced by
divine sanction, or rather by divine command, as well as by the
opinion of men—is the duty which, during the six days, is deeply
stamped on natures quite ready to receive it; and then something
is done towards obliterating the stamp, when, on the seventh day,
vengeance is interdicted.

A *priori*, it might be thought impossible that men should
continue through life holding two doctrines which are mutually
destructive. But their ability to compromise between conflicting
beliefs is very remarkable—remarkable, at least, if we suppose
them to put their conflicting beliefs side by side; not so remarkable if we recognize the fact that they do not put them side
by side. A late distinguished physicist, whose science and religion
seemed to his friends irreconcilable, retained both for the reason
that he deliberately refused to compare the propositions of the
one with those of the other. To speak in metaphor—when he
entered his oratory he shut the door of his laboratory; and when
he entered his laboratory he shut the door of his oratory. It is
because they habitually do something similar, that men live so
contentedly under this logically-indefensible compromise between their two creeds. As the intelligent child, propounding to
his seniors puzzling theological questions, and meeting many
rebuffs, eventually ceases to think about difficulties of which he
can get no solutions; so, a little later, the contradictions between
the things taught to him in school and in church, at first startling
and inexplicable, become by-and-by familiar, and no longer
attract his attention. Thus while growing up he acquires, in
common with all around him, the habit of using first one and

then the other of his creeds as the occasion demands; and at
maturity the habit has become completely established. Now he
enlarges on the need for maintaining the national honour, and
thinks it mean to arbitrate about an aggression instead of aveng-
ing it by war; and now, calling his servants together, he reads
a prayer in which he asks God that our trespasses may be for-
given as we forgive trespasses against us. That which he prays
for as a virtue on Sunday, he scorns as a vice on Monday.

The religion of amity and the religion of enmity, with the
emotions they respectively enlist, are important factors in sociological conclusions; and rational sociological conclusions can
be produced only when both sets of factors come into play. We
have to look at each cluster of social facts as a phase in a con-
tinuous metamorphosis. We have to look at the conflicting
religious beliefs and feelings included in this cluster of facts
as elements in this phase. We have to do more. We have to
consider as transitional, also, the conflicting religious beliefs and
feelings in which we are brought up, and which distort our
views not only of passing phenomena in our own society, but
also of phenomena in other societies and in other times; and
the aberrations they cause in our inferences have to be sought
for and rectified. Of these two religions taught us, we must
constantly remember that during civilization the religion of
enmity is slowly losing strength, [sic!] while the religion of
amity is slowly gaining strength. We must bear in mind that
at each stage a certain ratio between them has to be maintained.
We must infer that the existing ratio is only a temporary one;
and that the resulting bias to this or that conviction respecting
social affairs is temporary. And if we are to reach those unbiassed
convictions which form parts of the Social Science, we can do
it only by allowing for this temporary bias.

To see how greatly our opposite religions respectively per-
vert sociological beliefs, and how needful it is that the opposite
perversions they cause should be corrected, we must here contemplate the extremes to which men are carried, now by the
one and now by the other.

Karl Pearson

THE GRAMMAR OF SCIENCE *

Any way one cares to look at it, The Grammar of Science
*is a unique book in the development of science in gen-
eral and social science in particular. The two passages
selected serve, we think, to correct several very general
misconceptions of science which are as prevalent in our
time as they were in Pearson's.*

ESSENTIALS OF GOOD SCIENCE

I want the reader to appreciate clearly that science justifies itself
in its methods, quite apart from any serviceable knowledge it
may convey. We are too apt to forget this purely educational
side of science in the great value of its practical applications.
We see too often the plea raised for science that it is *useful
knowledge,* while philology and philosophy are supposed to have
small utilitarian or commercial value. Science, indeed, often
teaches us facts of primary importance for practical life; yet not
on this account, but because it leads us to classifications and
systems independent of the individual thinker, to sequences and
laws admitting of no play-room for individual fancy, must we
rate the training of science and its social value higher than those
of philology and philosophy. Herein lies the first, but of course
not the sole, ground for the popularisation of science. That form
of popular science which merely recites the results of investigations, which merely communicates *useful knowledge,* is from
this standpoint bad science, or no science at all. Let me recom-

* From Karl Pearson, *The Grammar of Science* (London, Adam and
Charles Black, 1911), pp. 9-12, 30-31. By permission of E. P. Dutton & Co.,
Inc. and of J. M. Dent & Sons Ltd., London.

mend the reader to apply this test to every work professing to
give a popular account of any branch of science. If any such
work gives a description of phenomena that appeals to his imagination rather than to his reason, then it is bad science. The first
aim of any genuine work of science, however popular, ought to
be the presentation of such a classification of facts that the
reader's mind is irresistibly led to acknowledge a logical se-
quence—a law which appeals to the reason before it captivates
the imagination. Let us be quite sure that whenever we come
across a conclusion in a scientific work which does not flow
from the classification of facts, or which is not directly stated
by the author to be an assumption, then we are dealing with
bad science. Good science will always be intelligible to the
logically trained mind, if that mind can read and translate the
language in which science is written. The scientific method is
one and the same in all branches, and that method is the method
of all logically trained minds. In this respect the great classics
of science are often the most intelligible of books, and if so,
are far better worth reading than popularisations of them written by men with less insight into scientific method. Works like
Darwin's *Origin of Species* and *Descent of Man,* Lyell's *Principles of Geology,* Helmholtz's *Sensations of Tone,* or Galton's
Natural Inheritance, can be profitably read and largely understood by those who are not specially trained in the several
branches of science with which these works deal.[1] It may need
some patience in the interpretation of scientific terms, in learning
the language of science, but like most cases in which a new language has to be learnt, the comparison of passages in which the
same word or term recurs, will soon lead to a just appreciation
of its true meaning. In the matter of language the descriptive
natural sciences such as geology or biology are more easily
accessible to the layman than the exact sciences such as algebra
or mechanics, where the reasoning process must often be clothed
in mathematical symbols, the right interpretation of which may
require months, if not years, of study. To this distinction between the descriptive and exact sciences I propose to return

---

[1] The list might be easily increased, for example by W. Harvey's
Anatomical Dissertation on the Motion of the Heart and Blood, and by
Faraday's *Experimental Researches.*

later, when we are dealing with the classification of the sciences.

I would not have the reader suppose that the mere perusal of some standard scientific work will, in my opinion, produce a scientific habit of mind. I only suggest that it will give some insight into scientific method and some appreciation of its value. Those who can devote persistently some four or five hours a week to the conscientious study of any *one* limited branch of science will achieve in the space of a year or two much more than this. The busy layman is not bound to seek about for some branch which will give him useful facts for his profession or occupation in life. It does not indeed matter for the purpose we have now in view whether he seek to make himself proficient in geology, or biology, or geometry, or mechanics, or even history or folklore, if these be studied scientifically. What is necessary is the *thorough* knowledge of some small group of facts, the recognition of their relationship to each other, and of the formulae or laws which express scientifically their sequences. It is in this manner that the mind becomes imbued with the scientific method and freed from individual bias in the formation of its judgments—one of the conditions, as we have seen, for ideally good citizenship. This first claim of scientific training, its education in method, is to my mind the most powerful claim it has to state support. I believe more will be achieved by placing instruction in pure science within the reach of all our citizens, than by any number of polytechnics devoting themselves to technical education, which does not rise above the level of manual instruction.

The Scope of Science

The reader may perhaps feel that I am laying stress upon *method* at the expense of material content. Now this is the peculiarity of scientific method, that when once it has become a habit of mind, that mind converts *all* facts whatsoever into science. The field of science is unlimited; its material is endless, every group of natural phenomena, every phase of social life, every stage of past or present development is material for science. *The unity of all science consists alone in its method, not in its material.*

SCIENCE AND THE IMAGINATION

. . . All great scientists have, in a certain sense, been great artists; the man with no imagination may collect facts, but he cannot make great discoveries. If I were compelled to name the Englishmen who during our generation have had the widest imaginations and exercised them most beneficially, I think I should put the novelists and poets on one side and say Michael Faraday and Charles Darwin. Now it is very needful to understand the exact part imagination plays in pure science. We can, perhaps, best achieve this result by considering the following proposition: Pure science has a further strong claim upon us on account of the exercise it gives to the imaginative faculties and the gratification it provides for the aesthetic judgment. The exact meaning of the terms "scientific fact" and "scientific law" will be considered in later chapters, but for the present let us suppose an elaborate classification of such facts has been made, and their relationships and sequences carefully traced. What is the next stage in the process of scientific investigation? Undoubtedly it is the use of the imagination. The discovery of some single statement, some brief *formula* from which the whole group of facts is seen to flow, is the work, not of the mere cataloguer, but of the man endowed with creative imagination. The single statement, the brief formula, the few words of which replace in our minds a wide range of relationships between isolated phenomena, is what we term a scientific *law*. Such a law, relieving our memory from the burden of individual sequences, enables us, with the minimum of intellectual fatigue, to grasp a vast complexity of natural or social phenomena. The discovery of law is therefore the peculiar function of the creative imagination. But this imagination has to be a *disciplined* one. It has in the first place to appreciate the whole range of facts, which require to be resumed in a single statement; and then when the law is reached—often by what seems solely the inspired imagination of genius—it must be tested and criticised by its discoverer in every conceivable way, till he is certain that the imagination has not played him false, and that his law is in real agreement with the whole group of phenomena which it resumes. Herein lies the key-note to the scientific use of the imagination. Hundreds of men have allowed their imagination to solve the universe, but the men who have contributed to our real understanding of natural phenomena have been those who were unstinting in their application of criticism to the product of their imaginations. It is such criticism which is the essence of the scientific use of the imagination, which is, indeed, the very life-blood of science.[1]

[1] *La critique est la vie de la science,* says Victor Cousin.

Robert Oppenheimer

A SCIENTIST
REFLECTS ON SCIENCE *

*Robert Oppenheimer, by almost any criterion of emi-
nence, is one of the towering scientific minds of our time.
A first-rate scientific intellect, in contrast to the much
more numerous over-specialized and myopic practitioners
of science, strives to see the forests as well as to examine
the trees. Oppenheimer's remarks in this reading, particularly when taken in conjunction with Pearson's,
should add considerably to the student's sophistication
about science in its broader contexts.*

The first characteristic of scientific knowledge today—a trivial and
pedestrian characteristic—is that its growth can be measured.
When I talk of "science" here I would like to use the word in
the broadest sense to include all man's knowledge of his history
and behavior, his knowledge, in fact, of anything that can be
talked of in an objective way so that people all over the world
can understand it, know what the scientist has done, reproduce
it, and find out if it is true or not. It is hard to measure the growth
of science defined in these terms in a sensible way but it can be
measured in fairly foolish ways.

One way of measuring science, for example, is to find out
how many people are engaged in it. I know a young historian of
science who has amused himself by counting the scientists of the

* Excerpt from Robert Oppenheimer, "The Tree of Knowledge,"
Harper's Magazine, vol. 217, no. 1301 (October, 1958), pp. 55-58. The
article as it appears in *Harper's Magazine* is a transcript of a talk given
by Dr. Oppenheimer before the International Press Institute in April, 1958.
By permission of the author.

last two centuries and he has found that their number has, quite accurately, doubled about every ten years. Professor Purcell of Harvard put the same conclusion another way the other day when he said, "Ninety per cent of all scientists are alive." This gives some notion of the changes involved.

I must, however, qualify this trend in two ways. First, it cannot continue, because if it went on for another century, then everyone would be a scientist—there would be nobody else left. So a kind of saturation is setting in and the rate of science's growth is slowing down. The second qualification is that what might be called the "stature" of science is not proportional to its volume; it may be proportional to the cube root of its volume or something like that. In short, every scientist is not a Newton and the proportion of Newtons among all scientists tends to decline as the number of people involved gets bigger.

Despite all qualifications, though, the fact remains that the growth in the number of people in science and the growth in firm knowledge—important, non-trivial knowledge of the kind that appears in learned journals and books—have been more or less parallel; and this growth will continue, although the increase in it is bound to taper off. The result is that nearly everything that is now known was not in any book when most of us went to school; we cannot know it unless we have picked it up since. This in itself presents a problem of communication that is nightmarishly formidable.

On the other hand, there is a more encouraging aspect of this scientific knowledge. As it grows, things, in some ways, get much simpler. They do not get simpler because one discovers a few fundamental principles which the man in the street can understand and from which he can derive everything else. But we do find an enormous amount of order. The world is not random and whatever order it has seems in large part "fit," as Thomas Jefferson said, for the human intelligence. The enormous variety of facts yields to some kind of arrangement, simplicity, generalization.

One great change in this direction—and it has not yet, I think, fully come to public understanding—is that we are beginning to see that the hard boundaries which once seemed to separate the parts of the natural world from each other are now yielding to some kind of inquiry. We are beginning to see ways across the gaps between the living and the dead, the physical and the mental.

Let me give just a few illustrations:

• It is probably not an accident, although it is not really understood, that the age of the earth—some six or seven billion years according to calculation by radioactive techniques—is very close to the period required for the most distant nebulae to recede into the furthest reaches of space. We can picturesquely define that time by saying that during it things were a lot closer together than they are now and the state of the material universe was very different. Some years ago the brilliant Russian biochemist Oparin suggested that when the atmosphere had no oxygen in it, certain conditions could have prevailed on earth under which life could have originated from inorganic matter. There has since been confirmation in Urey's laboratory and this hypothesis turns out to be true. Although mermaids and heroes do not walk out of the test tube, we do see that quite reasonable accounts of the origin of life are not too far from our grasp.

• The recent research on how the genetic mechanisms of all living material operate shows how certain proteins have special information-bearing properties—how they can store information and transmit it from one generation to another.[1]

• The study of how the nerve impulses from our sense organs to the brain can be modulated and altered by the perceptive apparatus of the animal—often it is an animal rather than a man—gives us some notion both of the unreliability of our sense impressions and of the subtlety of the relations between thought and the object of thought.

All these problems, which even in the nineteenth century seemed to obstruct the possibility of a unified view of the great arch of nature, are yielding to discovery; and in all science there is a pervasive, haunting sense that no part of nature is really irrelevant to any other.

Gay and Wonderful Mystery

But the model of science which results from all this investigation is entirely different from a model which would have seemed

[1] An account of this development, by F. H. C. Crick, appeared in *Scientific American*, September, 1957.

natural and understandable to the Greeks or the Newtonians. Although we do start from common human experience, as they did, we so refine what we think, we so change the meaning of words, we build up so distinctive a tradition, that scientific knowledge today is not an enrichment of the general culture. It is, on the contrary, the possession of countless, highly specialized communities who love it, would like to share it, would very much like to explain it, and who make some efforts to communicate it; but it is not part of the common human understanding. This is the very strange predicament to which the press addresses itself today and to which it can give, I believe, only a partial solution.

It would of course be splendid—and one often hears this—if we could say that while we cannot know the little details about the workings of atoms and proteins and the human psyche, we *can* know the fundamental principles of science. But I am afraid that this is only marginally true. The fundamentals of physics are defined in terms of words that refer to an experience that lay people have not had and that very few people have run across in their education.

For example, in my opinion, it is almost impossible to explain what the fundamental principle of relativity is about, and this is even more true of the quantum theory. It is only possible to use analogies, to evoke some sense of understanding. And as for the recent discovery—the very gay and wonderful discovery for which Dr. Yang and Dr. Lee were awarded the Nobel Prize—that nature has a preference for right-handed or left-handed screws in certain situations and is not indifferent to the handedness of the screw—to explain this is, I believe, quite beyond my capacity. And I have never heard anyone do it in a way that could be called an enrichment of culture.

To sum up the characteristics of scientific knowledge today, then, I would say that it is mostly new; it has not been digested; it is not part of man's common knowledge; it has become the property of specialized communities who may on occasion help one another but who, by and large, pursue their own way with growing intensity further and further from their roots in ordinary life.

We must always remember that, like most human accomplishments, the sciences have grown out of a long, accumulating experience of error, astonishment, invention, and understanding. Taken as a whole, they constitute a series of traditions; and these traditions—once largely common, now largely separate—are as essential to understanding a part of biology or astronomy or physics as the general human tradition is to the existence of civilized life. I know that a complete immersion in these many different, related, yet specific traditions is beyond the reach of any one person—that as things stand today, most of us are without any experience, really, in any. We have much in common from the simple ways in which we have learned to live and talk and work together. Out of this have grown the specialized disciplines like the fingers of the hand, united in origin but no longer in contact.

Practical Booby Traps

Now I am going to make a distinction which may seem arbitrarily sharp but which is I think important both to the learned community and the press. I have been talking until now about science as the things we have discovered about nature—incredible things and beautiful and astonishing, but defined, usually, not by any use to which they are put, but simply in terms of the ways in which they were found out. Pure science is thus inherently circumscribed but immensely revealing, showing as it does that left to itself, a man's imagination was not a patch on reality.

Seeking out this knowledge is one problem and I am not through with it. But the other problem is that, of course, this knowledge has practical consequences. On it is built the world we live in and the face of that world has been changed, probably more than in any other period of history, by the scientific revolution. Now these practical consequences, because they are intended in some day to be responsive to man's needs, can be talked about in an intelligible way. It is not necessary to know how a nucleus is put together, or what are the laws which determine its behavior, in order to explain what nuclear energy is all about. It may be very hard to explain it well because it involves human choices, options, decisions, prejudices. But I believe that it is no more difficult to write about nuclear energy than about where people go for a holiday. It is not much harder to write about nuclear weapons, except that, to the problems of human variety, there is added the problem of a very great deal of secrecy.

To take another example, it has not been hard to write about the use of vaccines in the prevention of disease and these can be described without elaborate theory. As a matter of fact the vaccines were discovered without much theoretical background and the atomic bomb was made before we had much idea what held nuclei together; we do not have very much idea today.

The press has done an admirable job in explaining these and other practical applications of science—I think it is aware that it has to do a much, much greater one. But there are, I think, some booby traps which stand in its way . . .

One of the simplest traps is that when technical people talk they always emphasize the fact that they are not sure. Sometimes, as in the case of knowing all the effects of radiation on life, we are not, in fact, sure, because experience takes so long to acquire. But usually the statement that we are not sure is more like the polite comment, "I don't want to bore you but . . ." Statements about scientific matters are not entirely sure—nothing is—but compared to politics they are so extremely sure as to be of a different order of certainty. If a scientist says he is not sure, pay attention to the limits within which he says this—the margin for error he insists on allowing. This margin will not be so wide. Within what limits we are uncertain about the genetic damages of radiation, for example, is not something to worry or wonder about. We know something of the effects on the genes. The differences of opinion over this question lie in quite a different field. They lie in conflicting assessments of the relative gravity of these damages and of other vaster dangers of total nuclear war.

A second trap to beware of is the strange fact that the words scientists use have taken on special meaning so that there is a confusing quality of punning when they discuss technical things and describe their aims. "Relativity" sounds like something that occurs in daily life; it is not. Scientists talk about the "adventure"

of science and they are right; but of course in the public mind
this is very likely to be identified with looking to see if the
other side of the moon is really there. Here the public is wrong.
The adventures of science are intellectual adventures, involving
discoveries of the inadequacy of our means of describing nature,
because it is so unfamiliar and strange. Space travel has, no
doubt, its value and virtue, but it is in no way related to the
great adventures of science. It would be, of course, if we could
go out two or three billion light-years and see what is going on
there, because it is hard to see that far with telescopes. But this
is not the same thing as the progress of human learning and
understanding.

President's Science Advisory Committee

SCIENTIFIC PROGRESS
AND EDUCATION *

Everywhere, it seems, in our time, there is discussion of the distinction between what is called "basic" research and other kinds, upon both of which, of course, the maintenance of science rests. The study from which this reading was taken was prepared by a group of distinguished scientists and educators commissioned to examine a number of features of basic research, particularly the relationship between federal government and the universities, a relationship which is much more intimate than many people realize. Students particularly, whether or not planning careers in science, should find this reading not only of sociological but of personal import.

Basic research is the cutting of paths through the unknown. As most of us know today, it is the pacesetter for technology, and the raw material of invention. Its growth can be assisted, and its general value can be confidently asserted, but it depends, in the end, on the imaginative powers and scientific skills of the men who do it. Basic research is as hard as it is exciting, and while it contributes enormously to the national welfare, what usually moves the scientist is not so much this practical consequence of his labor as the simple but powerful urge to know how nature works. A free society can honor the scientist's curiosity without forgetting his social value.

* *Scientific Progress, The Universities, and The Federal Government,* President's Science Advisory Committee (Washington, D.C., U. S. Government Printing Office, 1960), pp. 4-6. (Italics by the editors.)

Because basic research is aimed at understanding rather than at practical results, the layman sometimes assumes that it is entirely abstract and theoretical, and that only when it becomes a matter of industrial development does it "come down to earth." This is a false notion, and its falsity becomes increasingly clear with time. *Indeed, one striking characteristic of our scientific age has been the disappearance of the barriers between pure and applied science.* Not only are we finding important technological applications for mathematical and scientific knowledge which was formerly thought of as abstract and "useless," but the advance of technology has both generated new problems in pure science and provided new tools with which such science can be advanced more effectively. The development of the techniques and hardware for radar during the war, for example, gave the physicist and the chemist a new and refined tool for investigating the properties of solids and of chemical compounds. Conversely, the extensive use of this tool in basic science has opened the way to entirely new techniques in electronics. Similarly, the development of large-scale electronic computers has led engineers to find practical uses for some of the most abstruse and "impractical" branches of higher mathematics, while the understanding of the techniques of using computers has, on the other hand, given us deeper insight into some aspects of the behavior of complex biological and social systems. *Basic and applied science today are distinguished less by method and content than by motivation.* Part of the strength of American science stems from close intellectual intercourse between basic and applied scientists. Very often, indeed, the same man can be both "pure scientist" and "engineer," as he works on different problems or on different parts of one problem. We do not believe in any artificial separation between basic and applied research or between science and engineering. The fact that a scientific advance is useful does not make it unscientific.

Graduate education for scientists is usually seen as what comes after the B.A. and before the Ph.D. For us it is this, but also more, and in our view any definition in terms of an interval between two degrees obscures much more than it clarifies. We are using the term here to mean that part of education which seeks to turn a young man or woman into a scientist. *By the word "scientist" we mean someone who is fit to take part in basic research, to learn without a teacher, to discover and attack significant problems not yet solved, to show the nature of this process to others*—someone, in short, who is equipped to spend a lifetime in the advancement of science, to the best of his ability.

It is a fundamental contention of this report that the process of graduate education and the process of basic research *belong together* at every possible level. We believe that the two kinds of activity reinforce each other in a great variety of ways, and that each is weakened when carried on without the other. We think also that this proposition has substantial implications for the policy of both the Federal Government and the universities. Because the proposition is so central to our argument, we must try to demonstrate it thoroughly.

In one sense, it is almost self-evident. If graduate education aims at making scientists, and if inquiry into what is unknown is the moving principle of all science, it is not surprising that experience of this kind of inquiry should be essential in graduate education. Clearly such experience is best obtained in association with others who have had it or are having it themselves. The apprentice scientist learns best when he learns in an atmosphere of active research work. It is true that only a minority of those who receive a Ph.D. in science continue their subsequent careers in basic research. The majority go on to applied research in industry or to teaching in college where research opportunities are limited. (Even in the universities many scientists are not active in research.) Nevertheless, such experience as all graduate students should have with basic research is highly important. In all forms of scientific work a man's effectiveness is multiplied when he has that depth of understanding of his subject that comes only with the experience of working at a research problem.

But if all this is so, it does not seem to be fully recognized in the standard practices of most universities and Federal agencies. For as we are describing it, the process of graduate education depends on "research" just as much as upon "teaching"—indeed the two are essentially inseparable—and there is a radical error in trying to think of them as different or opposite forms of activity. From the point of view of the graduate student, the teaching and the research of his professor are, at the crucial point which defines the whole, united. What he learns is not opposite from research; it *is* research. Of course many necessary parts of a scientist's education have little to do with research, and obviously also for many professors there must be a gap between teaching a standard graduate course and working at one's own problems. Moreover, many good teachers—men who keep up with the new work in their subject and communicate its meaning clearly to their students—are not themselves engaged in research. Yet we insist on the central point; the would-be scientist must learn what it is like to do science, and this, which is research, is the most important thing he can be "taught."

So far we have been arguing that graduate education requires the experience of basic research. What happens when we turn the matter around, and ask whether basic research must be carried on only in conjunction with graduate education? Here the answer cannot be so categorical. Though our general conviction is that a fundamentally reciprocal relation does exist, it is clear that research of outstanding quality is often carried on in isolation from teaching and indeed quite outside the universities. While the great teacher of graduate students is almost invariably a research man too, there are many notable scientists who have as little as possible to do with teaching. First-rate industrial and governmental laboratories with commitments to specific programs are necessarily separated in some measure from teaching of a conventional sort. Thus basic research can be and is carried on without much connection to graduate education.

Yet in the long run it is dangerous to separate research in any field entirely from education. If a research field is to be attractive to good young men, it ordinarily needs roots in the universities. The pool of graduate students in our universities is the pool from which the scientists of the future must come. These young people do not easily study what is not taught; they do not often learn the meaning of research which does not exist in their environment. A scientific field which has no research life in the universities is at a grave disadvantage in recruiting new members. As learning and teaching require research, so research, in the end, cannot be sustained without teaching. Hence it is always important for research installations to maintain effective connections with students.

Robert Bierstedt

SOCIOLOGY
AND HUMANE LEARNING *

Robert Bierstedt is one of our most literate and provocative critics of the present condition of sociology as a discipline. In a series of articles and at least one book, he has from time to time reminded us that some of our professional folkways need to be re-examined periodically. The following reading is an excerpt from his presidential address before the Eastern Sociological Society in which he pleads, in language which is at times poetic, for a more broad appreciation of what the sociological tradition has to offer—for the retention of the humanities tradition without necessarily disparaging the more narrowly scientific effort.

. . . For it seems to be the case that we confront in sociology today the rather odd paradox that the significance of our research varies inversely with the precision of the methods employed. Or, as [Robert] Redfield put it in another paper on this subject: "The emphasis on formal method sometimes carries the social scientist into exercises in which something not very important is done very well." [1]

Now many of us may accept these consequences with equanimity on the ground that conclusions of modest proportions

* Excerpt from Robert Bierstedt, "Sociology and Humane Learning," *American Sociological Review*, Vol. 25, No. 1 (Feb., 1960), pp. 5-9. Presidential address read at the annual meeting of the Eastern Sociological Society, April, 1959. Used by permission of the author and the *American Sociological Review*.

[1] "Social Science Among the Humanities," *Measure*, 1 (Winter, 1950), p. 62.

are the price we pay for precision, and that precision, in turn, is one of the most fundamental requirements of the scientific enterprise. For my own part I have to express what is doubtless a minority view and say that I regard this situation with regret. Is sociology to be a niggling business, doing the easy thing because it is accurate, and avoiding the difficult thing because it is imprecise? We have often been told, and by numerous hostile critics, that sociology is a mean and petty science, pursued by people who take delight in counting the privies in Pittsburgh and discovering, with the most versatile of techniques, that people with high incomes spend more money than people with low incomes. I exaggerate, of course, and it would be invidious in any event to select examples from the literature. But it is distressing to think that sociology can be associated with the solution of problems of a trivial kind and that the more precise our research becomes the more our science resembles the deaf man in Tolstoy, muttering answers to questions that no one has asked him. . . .

Our preoccupation with method has still other consequences, not yet mentioned. It frequently dominates our inquiries and determines the kinds of questions we address to society; that is, the method becomes the independent variable, the problem the dependent one. Instead of setting for ourselves tasks of large dimensions and then devising methods appropriate to their solution, we are apt to ask only those questions that are answerable in terms of methods presently available. We have even been invited to forego those larger problems of human society that occupied our ancestors in the history of social thought and to seek instead what T. H. Marshall called, in his inaugural lecture at the University of London, "stepping stones in the middle distance," and other sociologists since, "theories of the middle range." But what an anemic ambition this is! Shall we strive for half a victory? Where are the visions that enticed us into the world of learning in the first place? I had always thought that sociologists too knew how to dream and that they believed with Browning that a man's reach should exceed his grasp.

But enough of criticism. Some of my comparisons, as you no doubt recognize, may be meretricious and all perhaps are exaggerated. They may be meretricious in the sense that it is always easy to compare the brilliant and profound philosopher in sociology with the dull and mediocre statistician, the creative theorist with the unimaginative researcher. Such comparisons are as illicit as the reverse would be—the ingenious and versatile researcher *versus* the confused or unintelligible theorist. Nor do I have any intention of resurrecting the ancient methodological argument, the one that raged in the pages of our books and journals a couple of decades ago, as to whether or not sociology is or ought to be a science. Let me emphasize for the record my own conviction that sociology ought to be as scientific as it possibly can be, that it ought to conform to all the canons of scientific inquiry, and that conclusions ought to be public and publicly verifiable. When I say that sociology ought to be a science, however, I do not imply that it should be *only* a science. I think we ought to take much more seriously and literally the view that sociology can also serve as a bridge between the sciences and the humanities and that in a very important sense it belongs to the realm of humane letters. . . .

In this connection I should like to introduce another somewhat wayward notion. We have always insisted, with a proper bow to Francis Bacon, upon the elimination of bias in our inquiries and have emphasized the need for as complete an objectivity as it is humanly possible to attain. We have often suggested that in the social sciences, as contrasted with the physical sciences, objectivity is a condition to be achieved and not one initially given in our scientific situation and that this fact creates greater difficulties for the sociologist, for example, than for his colleagues in physics, chemistry, and biology, and requires perhaps a more alert responsibility. We have realistically recognized, of course, that a complete objectivity, though a methodological *desideratum,* is nevertheless for any individual a psychological impossibility and that what we should hope for is not a total absence of bias but rather an overt awareness of it. Finally, we have admitted in our wiser moments that behind every great sociologist there stands a social philosopher and that not even the scientific sociologist can ultimately escape the ethical and political consequences of his own approach to the problems of society.

All of this is to the good. And yet, I want to suggest the alternative possibility that objectivity may not be as desirable a criterion as it is commonly thought to be. For certain purposes, including the kind of sociological research I have been advocating by implication, it might be preferable to utilize what I shall call "the theoretic bias." The theoretic bias would enable us to push a particular interpretation of social phenomena just as far as it is reasonable to go in our effort to shed illumination upon it.[2] It would candidly employ exaggeration as an heuristic device. In examining the problems of social change, for example, an objective approach is apt to be a pallid and unsuccessful one. These problems are not in fact amenable to solution with methods currently available. It would seem to be much better, therefore, to take a single factor and to push it to an extreme as a possible mode of interpretation. Thus, Marx used the theoretic bias to support the role of the economic factor, Buckle the geographic factor, Freud the psychological, Weber the ideological, Durkheim the sociological (in a special sense), and so on. Each one of these thinkers was lured into excess by his enthusiasm for his own bias and each was surely guilty of exaggeration. The greatest thinkers, however, have not been the neutral and objective ones, but those who have turned their biases to good account. And each biased conclusion, of course, is open to refinement, modification, and correction by others of a contrary kind, so that the outcome over the course of time is, if not knowledge in a narrow sense, a much more sophisticated appreciation of the problem than would otherwise be possible. I am inclined to wonder, in short, whether in our assault upon some of the larger problems of sociology biased theses may not serve as better than objective hypotheses. . . .

I have been constrained in these sentences to emphasize that scientific method, as important and indeed as necessary as it is, does not exhaust the resources of scholarship in sociology and that, as we aspire for significance, objectivity and the pur-

[2] The role of reason in sociological research has received insufficient attention in our literature. On this subject see the thoughtful essay by Reinhard Bendix, *Social Science and the Distrust of Reason* (Berkeley and Los Angeles, University of California Press, 1951), esp. pp. 26-42. See also Robert Bierstedt, "A Critique of Empiricism in Sociology," *American Sociological Review*, 14 (October, 1949), pp. 584-592.

suit of truth, may have less to offer us than the theoretic bias and the search for cogency. You may of course reject the criticisms that led to this conclusion and ignore the exhortations. But I should still maintain, in brief conclusion, that sociology has an honorable place in the realm of humane letters and that it belongs with the liberal arts as well as with the sciences. We have seldom been able to escape the public belief that it is the principal business of sociology to solve social problems; and the identification of our discipline with such problems is too well known to require comment. That sociology might also have something to do with culture in the narrower and non-sociological sense of intellectual cultivation seems seldom to have occurred to anyone, including sociologists.

I invite your attention, therefore, to the fact that sociology, like the other arts, is one of the ornaments of the human mind, that its literature extending from Plato to our contemporaries is in a great and humane tradition, that sociology—like all of the liberal arts—liberates us from the provincialisms of time and place and circumstance, that the social order is a study worthy of a free man, and that society itself, like every other thing that has ever agitated the restless and inquisitive mind of man, is a fit and dignified subject of inquiry.

May I say finally that we are easily misled. "It is not the lofty sails but the unseen wind that moves the ship." It is not the methods and the concepts that move our sociology along, but memory and desire—the memory that other men in other times have also asked questions about society and the desire that our answers, in our time, will be better than theirs.

Business Week

SOCIOLOGISTS
INVADE THE PLANT *

It is increasingly being recognized that sociological research has had practical applications in a variety of fields. Sociologists are currently doing research in the employ of the armed forces, the State Department, and, of course, many private corporations, all of whom have problems to be solved for which the special techniques and knowledge of the sociologist are required. The following reading first appeared in Business Week. *It constitutes a summary of some of the kinds of work which have been done in the business world and gives something of an indication of the extent of this application.*

The sociologists snooping through the factory—listening to gossip, watching how the workers behave at work, at lunch, and in coffee breaks, eyeing the finished product for its consumer appeal —represent a newly developed breed.

They have turned their back on the "social problems" of crime and broken homes that were their original domain. Now they are part of a fast-growing field of industrial sociology—and they are invading the business world because business has invited them in through the front door.

• *Last In*——But the invitation has been long in coming. One by one, the other academic disciplines which school administrators like to call "social studies" have scraped out a place for

* Reprinted from the March 21, 1959 issue of *Business Week* by special permission. Copyright © 1959 by the McGraw-Hill Publishing Company, Inc., pp. 95-96, 101.

themselves in the business community. First to come were the full-fledged economists, with doctorates in their hands. It has been estimated that 30 years ago fewer than 100 economists graced the corporate payrolls. Today there are thousands.

After World War II, fresh from wide-ranging experience in the armed forces, came the psychologists. With their background in personality rating, they offered advice on personnel selection. Their delvings into sensory perception gave them a background for advising on product and package design. Their studies of the inner broodings of the human mind provided new tools for ad-men, put such terms as "motivational research" into common use.

Now come the sociologists (and their first cousins, the social psychologists and the anthropologists), scouting along somewhat the same paths, but with a different set of field glasses and charting equipment. And businessmen, far from discouraging their ardor, are handing out money to them and turning them loose to find answers to numerous business problems.

I. What Do They Do?

But what do the sociologists have to offer that business can't get from the economists or the psychologists? The sociologists' specialty is the study, not of man as an individual, but of the way he behaves in groups, and the forms and functions of the groups themselves. And their particular contribution to business is just that—their knowledge of how groups act and how they differ from one another.

Economists, for example, chart the buying power of consumer groups, and similar matters; sociologists delve into their value patterns—the things that make various consumer types, urban or rural, upper or lower bracket, white or blue collar, responsive or hostile to certain products or appeals. Pajama makers, for example, learned something about styling from a study by the Bureau of Applied Social Research; they found that the kind of virile styling that sold high-priced outfits in men's stores didn't go over well in middle-priced lines, where women do the buying in department stores. Sociologists can come up with some similar answers regarding behavior of workers in specific groups.

In these probings, the sociologists tread a bit on the toes of market researchers on one side and psychologists on the other. But businessmen find the sociologists have a special contribution to make, too.

• *How Many and How Much?*——No one is willing to guess just how many of the 6,000-plus sociologists in the U.S. today are regular corporate employees:

The American Sociological Society, in fact, has just launched a study to find the answer. In 1950, 5% of its members worked for industry. Since then, the society is sure, the percentage "has been growing greatly—but we don't know just how much."

Nor will anyone estimate how much business spends on such social research, on its own and through grants to universities, beyond the guess that the total "runs into millions." But here's one indicator: In six years of collecting funds for sociological research, the Foundation for Research on Human Behavior has rounded up $226,000 from 27 companies, ranging from Detroit Edison Co. through Aluminum Co. of America to Federated Department Stores, Inc. And these 27 have promised regular annual gifts.

• *What For?*——Sometimes businessmen have turned to the sociologists in desperation, or as a last resort when nobody else could come up with the right answer.

A dictation machine maker, for example, wanted to find out why it was having a tough time breaking into big companies. Social researchers turned up this anwer: Secretaries feared the machines would turn them into little more than pool typists, with no direct contact with the boss; and the boss felt that dictating to his own secretary was a symbol of status.

Usually, though, the sociologizing is more in the nature of a forward look to see how things can be improved. In some corporate circles it has become a fashion, and there the sociologists can carve out their own projects. Most of the work contracted out to universities is more general in application, not aimed at finding some specific cure.

• *Sales Aids*——One of the earliest sociological research units organized to deal with business problems was the Bureau of

Applied Social Research set up at Columbia University in 1937 by Dr. Paul Lazarsfeld. In the 1940's, it did research largely for advertising media, picking out the influential groups in communities and showing how the pattern of influence changed with the idea or product involved. The media gladly underwrote the research, grabbed at it to persuade the potential advertiser that theirs was the best channel for his product story.

Lately the advertiser himself has jumped in. Two Iowa State College sociologists charted the pattern of adoption for new farm products—the kind of people most receptive to innovation and those who would wait longest, where they got their information, how long they were likely to wait. Eli Lilly and Co. used this to map a campaign for a new beef cattle hormone feed additive. It made no special appeal to the self-starters who go looking for new products at experimental stations, directed its first farm magazine campaign at the middle-of-the-roaders, delayed until a year later its local farm paper campaign aimed at the bulk of the prospects. Use each year has come within 2% of predicted sales.

On similar lines, Monsanto Chemical Co. is working with university researchers to see how consumers who sent in a coupon for a free sample of a new product compare with a cross-section of all potential users.

• *Personnel*—The social researchers have put employees as well as consumers under their microscopes. Companies sending employees overseas have called in anthropologists to brief them on local customs and traditions—to avoid such missteps as chucking an Iranian baby under the chin and thus, according to superstition, putting an evil eye on him.

At home, Esso Standard Oil Co. runs training sessions, based on National Training Laboratories techniques, to teach supervisors about group dynamics. Men are brought together—say, at the Gulf Hills dude ranch in Mississippi—but with little advance briefing on what it's all about. As they begin to interact, choose leaders, decide what to do, the training leader points out how the group has made decisions and various members have influenced it. The idea is to make more effective group members—important in this committee-run company.

In other companies, sociologists have looked at internal

communications, tracing how a rumor spreads through a plant, for instance; or tried to determine the corporate climate that best fosters creativity, or to "type" company stockholders so management can reach them more effectively.

Sometimes the sociologists' contribution is something more obvious—like telling the company that employee group discussions of a supervisor's shortcomings would be more honest if the supervisor wasn't present.

• *Answers*—At times the sociologists retreat behind a scientific façade and give the company "we just report the findings, you must interpret them yourself" routine. But frequently businessmen do get a specific answer about what to do—the pajama makers, for example, got and accepted a suggestion to make colors "bright but not too loud." The worried dictation machine maker got one, too—to set up, with much pomp, a "training institute" for girls getting dictation machines—but turned it down.

II. Two-Way Street

With sociology getting a business reputation, tomorrow's businessmen themselves are likely to come to their jobs with more training in the subject. The schools of business are getting on the band wagon, putting more social studies into their curricula.

• The University of Pennsylvania's Wharton School of Finance & Commerce has long had a required course in "society as a system of interdependent human relationships."

• Columbia University's Graduate School of Business, a revamped program being introduced next fall, will have a required course dubbed, "Human Behavior in Organization," aimed at enabling a manager to assess the effects on group behavior of proposed changes in organization or technology.

• The University of Chicago's School of Business now includes "behavior science" as one of the four "basic disciplines" for each student.

• The Ford Foundation has given money to business schools at five state universities for work in social sciences, and makes funds available for business school faculty members to take time off to study these fields.

• *Reserve Action*—Social researchers, too, are becoming

more interested in business. The American Sociological Society currently lists 115 research projects going on in industrial sociology—up from 84 four years ago. Its September meeting will probably have twice as many papers on the subject as there were only five years ago.

The Ford Foundation has financed work on such business problems as the effect of a new man in a top job, or the relationship between a big corporation and the cities where it has plants. Another $125,000 has been set aside to help graduate students' research on business organization.

Roscoe C. Hinkle, Jr. and Gisela J. Hinkle

SOCIOLOGY:
AN EMERGING DISCIPLINE *

Roscoe C. and Gisela J. Hinkle are careful and competent students of sociological theory. The small book, The Development of Modern Sociology, *from which this reading was taken is an attempt to trace the historical roots of modern sociology. The following reading is the concluding few pages of that book. It touches not only upon the institutional structure of society in our time and upon the uses to which sociology is put, but also touches upon some of its philosophical assumptions.*

Today American sociology is a firmly established social-scientific discipline possessing its own body of knowledge, concepts, and theories. In contrast to the early years, there are now over four thousand professional sociologists, more and more with urban backgrounds, and employed throughout all regions of the country in all types of academic institutions and in numerous private industries and governmental agencies. So many new sociological periodicals, books, regional and special associations have appeared and the field has become so differentiated and its methods so specialized that the sociology student as a rule finds little time during his professional training to become proficient in other disciplines as well.

While many of the present subfields are outgrowths of the social problems studied during the formative era—for example, criminology, family and marriage, old age, and social and personal disorganization—new specialties have emerged. Some of these new areas, such as communication and public opinion, small-group study, industrial sociology, and social stratification, reflect the new social conditions and relationships of mass society. Other subfields, such as sociology of health, the study of the child, and analyses of authority and leadership, have been more specifically related to the growth of interdisciplinary and large-scale research.

Sociologists have specialized their research techniques without having entirely resolved the older controversy between the quantitative-mathematical and qualitative approaches. Today the initial formulation of the research problem usually specifies the type of procedure to be used, whether attitude scales, questionnaires, and census data or interviews, participant observation, and case-history analysis, or combinations of two or more of these.

As field differentiation and specialization occurred the basic elements of the sociological point of view evidenced some notable modifications and continuities. Since many of these continuities are likely to persist, they embody some clues as to the prospects of the future developments of American sociology.

Sociologists still assume that there is a universal similarity about all human behavior which can eventually be codified as a system of universal interrelated laws. Seeking to construct such a logical system of laws, recent systematic theory differs from earlier endeavors which assumed that investigations of empirical phenomena would reveal laws inherent in nature. Yet the empirical preoccupation so characteristic of the second era of American sociology has not been relinquished entirely. Contemporary sociologists generally follow an approach intermediate to "pure theory" and "raw empiricism" in their quest for the scientific laws of society. It seems likely that at least some of the popularity of Merton's "theories of the middle range" stems from their articulate expression of this scientific approach.

In their efforts to establish laws of human behavior, social structure, and change sociologists use methods patterned after other social and natural sciences, at least implicitly. They tend to emphasize quantification by using measurement and statistical techniques, to approximate experimentation by constructing research designs, and to interrelate their activities by formulating hypotheses drawn from existent principles, generalizations, and laws. Sociologists generally avoid the use of historical materials because historical data are conceived to be essentially unique rather than repetitive and general and consequently unsuitable to measurement or experimentation. Theories of social change are, therefore, often ahistorical and devoid of cultural concreteness.

While sociology is still justified by its usefulness, its direct relationship to humanitarian reformism and meliorism, as based on the rationale of the belief in progress, has been replaced by an explicit or implicit utilitarianism. Nevertheless, there is the implication that such instrumentalism will operate for the common good which, as a consequence of the several national crises, has been equated with national welfare. In order to be useful, sociological research focuses particularly on the goal of prediction and control.

During all three eras of American sociology its individualism, as it has been termed in this study, is perhaps its most significant characteristic. The feeling, knowing, and willing of individuals—though limited by cultural prescriptions and social controls—are taken to be the ultimate source of human interaction, social structure, and social change. A deterministic explanation inimical to this basic postulate of voluntarism finds, and no doubt will find in the future, few protagonists. A sociology of knowledge, for instance, which maintains a strict causal relationship between a specific form of social existence or class position and knowledge is unlikely to gain many adherents among American sociologists. Indeed, most sociological generalizations are specifically formulated as probability statements, thereby reserving a limited amount of freedom for the individual to deviate from the rule or law.

Social behavior is interpreted voluntaristically. Social structures are real only as they are products of individuals in interaction. The social action theory's emphasis on the intentions and goal-orientations of individuals illustrates this viewpoint. Most American sociologists phrase their research problems from the perspective of individual behavior and generally reinterpret more holistic approaches so that they coincide with this individualism. Consequently, neither Durkheim's notion of society as an entity *sui generis* nor Marx's interpretation of social stratification in terms of economic relations and consequent class consciousness has been accepted in American sociology in spite of widespread familiarity with these ideas.

Though influenced by changing American social conditions and crises and the growth and specialization of the discipline itself, modern American sociology has thus retained a basic homogeneity of viewpoint. Future developments will probably require investigations into as yet unknown areas of social life. But judging by the events of the past and current trends, American sociologists will be likely to explain such behavior, social organization, and change by universal laws based on the motivation of individuals in interaction.

Part Two

CULTURE

Those scholars and literati who like to erect line fences between the various so-called branches of learning have sometimes insisted that the study of culture "belongs" chiefly, if not exclusively, to cultural anthropology. What they miss is that concepts derived from property rights in the practical world do not have any real counterpart in the scholarly realm. In the world of ideas there can be no real poachers. Any realm belongs to him who cultivates it, for by his fruits he is known. So while we are mindful that by some conceptions of the matter the study of culture belongs perhaps chiefly to the anthropologist, and freely acknowledge the many contributions of professional anthropologists to its emerging sophistication, not many sociologists are able to do either theoretical or practical work without express or tacit use of the culture idea. It makes little difference whether the word *culture* is used, the *idea* of social heritage, an all-pervasive man-made set of specifications for behavior, is a concept which is central to almost all contemporary professional thinking about human behavior.

One of the earliest thinkers who has left an indelible stamp not only upon our sociological language but also on the thoughtways of social scientists is William Graham Sumner. His classic work *Folkways* [1] (1904) consists of a number of theories which he derived from empirical studies of people in various societies and times. One of the central ideas in his book which has lived and become almost a household word among ed-

[1] William Graham Sumner, *Folkways*, (Boston, Ginn and Company, 1904).

ucated people is the concept, "the mores." Sumner distinguished between folkways, mores, law, and other kinds of institutionalized practices, but the differences, it seems to us, are less important than the pervading similarities. Sometimes the text book definitions in which authors have paraphrased Sumner have been a bit too "pat." It should be refreshing to read what Sumner originally said on the subject (Page 54).

Everyone who studies anthropology or sociology learns at the outset the cliche: "culture is learned." Over a quarter of a century of teaching this concept to students has resulted in a conviction that the phraseology is learned far better than is the idea. Often there remains a lurking semi-conscious notion that, while some things are, to be sure, learned, the "deep down things" in personality, because they are so immutable, "must" spring from some other source, probably the biological. John Gillin in his usual readable fashion addresses himself to the *evidence* that culture is learned (Page 59). He directs attention back to the sources and spells out the logic for this now universally accepted (that is, among social scientists) proposition.

It has been said that the last thing which a creature living in the sea would discover would be water. Similarly, it could be observed that probably the last thing which the untrained mind would consider as the source of its content would be language. The role of language, not simply as a "medium of communication" but as a *source of personality content,* is underestimated by practically everybody, including sometimes distinguished scholars in a variety of fields. The essay on language, prepared especially for this volume (page 61) brings together some of the leading concepts which have evolved in the anthropological and social-psychological study of language.

One of the most common misunderstandings about culture, which derives probably from the way in which some behavior scientists have written and talked, is the tacit notion that as a blueprint for behavior it is consistent and clearcut. Nothing could be further from the truth. Actually all cultures, including our own, are fraught with innumerable ambiguities, inconsistencies, and contradictions. Part of this built-in chaos for Americans is due to what is called "cultural pluralism," that is, the people in our society, having come from a variety of cultures, still retain a considerable amount of the imported culture and hence there is a plural, rather than a single, set of cultural norms. But cultural inconsistencies and contradictions are also indigenous to each of the separate sub-cultures. Two papers are addressed to this problem, the first, "Our Schizoid Culture" by Read Bain, deals with the question in a general way (Page 69). The second paper, by Robert S. Lynd (page 78), narrows the focus somewhat and concentrates chiefly on ideological elements to show that the themes by which we live, which comprise the "American Creed," form by no means a coherent unity.

One of the recent emphases in the study of human behavior has been the emergence of a specialization called the study of "national character." A number of works, such as Ruth Benedict's *The Chrysanthemum and the Sword* [2] and Geoffrey Gorer's *The American People*,[3] are widely known. A great deal of work of a technical and precise nature has gone into this field of endeavor. The objective, however, has been essentially the same, namely to try to discover the central ideologies and deeper "character structures" of the "typical" personality in a given society (or culture). Obviously this involves a high level of generality and it is precisely at this point that some of the studies have proved less than convincing. The resultant picture is so generalized that to many people in the society which is being described, the emergent portrait does not seem quite real. Nor does it often make much difference if the portrait is fashioned from the inside, that is, by someone indigenous to the culture, or by an outsider, that is, a visiting social

[2] (Boston, Houghton-Mifflin & Co., 1946.)
[3] (New York, W. W. Norton and Company, Inc., 1948.)

scientist who may have the advantage of less ethno-
centrism but also has less experience. The excerpt from
Don Martindale on American character (page 82),
from the preface to his book *American Social Structure,*
presents a portrait of Americans with which probably
some Americans won't agree. But the perceptions of the
people recorded therein, one a poet and the other a
social scientist, can hardly be dismissed as not at least
worthy of thoughtful consideration. Some of these
"slants" on American society are sure to provide interest, even if accepted with reservations.

All culture is not ideological. Or, as some theorists
prefer to put it, some of the ideology becomes embodied
in material things, hence the familiar phrase, "material
culture." Particularly in contemporary Western society
there is a pervasive phenomenon which has become so
much a part and parcel of life that it is taken for granted
—technology. The late William F. Ogburn, a lifelong
student of technology and social change, discusses
(page 88) how persons in different positions in society
"come at" technology. The meanings which it has not
only vary but they vary with respect to the *function*
of technology to persons in various positions.

Perhaps the most important aspect of culture,
though not discussed directly in any of the readings in
this section, is treated in a number of others (for example, pages 229, 242, 248, 274, 284, 288, and 300),
namely the cardinal and ever baffling fact of *cultural
change.* Some theorists have gone so far as to define
culture as "a set of problem solving devices" for the
human. Putting the matter in this way, the inevitability
of change is better understood. So often, change is regarded as a defeat for the time-honored way of doing
or thinking. This leads to the unfortunate consequent
view that the normal condition of human existence is
constancy. To the tradition-minded this point of view
may be comfortable psychologically and may serve certain practical ends in politics or economics or morality,
but the proponents of traditional orientation always fight

a losing battle. They win some skirmishes now and then, to be sure, and the tactics for delaying action are sometimes quite ingenious, but, as the cliche goes, no one has for long held back the hands on the clock of time.

So here we have a curious paradox—the inevitability of change and the widespread prejudice against it. Why is this so? Why do human beings spend so much time and effort and suffer so much heartache trying to do the impossible? One can identify many reasons and together they may answer our question. Perhaps there is something inescapable about the psychology of simple habit. Then, of course, there is vested interest—for some there seems to be more to gain by retaining the old rather than embracing the new. There is also an inherent conflict between the nature of culture and the nature of society. The latter requires orderliness in order that it exist. In fact, social structure (or society itself) is often defined, as Robin Williams, Jr.[4] does, as the recurrent and therefore predictable uniformities in human behavior. Now, if culture is a set of problem-solving devices and man is an intelligent animal, he will presumably devise new, not necessarily better, ways of solving problems, and he will also find new problems to be solved. Thus, built into his life is an inescapable battle between the practical requirements of the social order, which dictates stability and continuity and predictability, and active intelligence which is the perpetual source of innovation in thought and deed. Man can thus be no automaton, despite the efforts of some to make him so, and the "social order," about which some write with dripping sentimentality, can at best be only a relative and partial measure of man's condition.

[4] *American Society* (New York, Alfred A. Knopf, Inc., 1951).

William Graham Summer

THE MORES *

Folkways is almost universally acknowledged to be one of the few top-drawer classics in the American sociological tradition. Its author, William Graham Sumner, was a professor in the Divinity School at Yale. His "research" consisted of a collection of reports by travelers and writers of the customs of far away peoples. He formulated, however, a considerable amount of theory concerning these collections of data. He also formulated some of the basic concepts which are still central in sociological thinking, among them the mores. The following excerpts are part of the development of his ideas and contain some of his theory about the mores.

66. *More exact definition of the mores.* We may now formulate a more complete definition of the mores. They are the ways of doing things which are current in a society to satisfy human needs and desires, together with the faiths, notions, codes, and standards of well living which inhere in those ways, having a genetic connection with them. By virtue of the latter element the mores are traits in the specific character (ethos) of a society or a period. They pervade and control the ways of thinking in all the exigencies of life, returning from the world of abstractions to the world of action, to give guidance and to win revivification. "The mores are, before any beginning of reflection, the regulators of the political, social, and religious behavior of the individual. Conscious reflection is the worst enemy of the mores, because mores begin unconsciously and pursue unconscious pur-

* William Graham Sumner, *Folkways* (Boston, Ginn & Co., 1904), paragraphs 66, 68, 80 and 83. Used by permission.